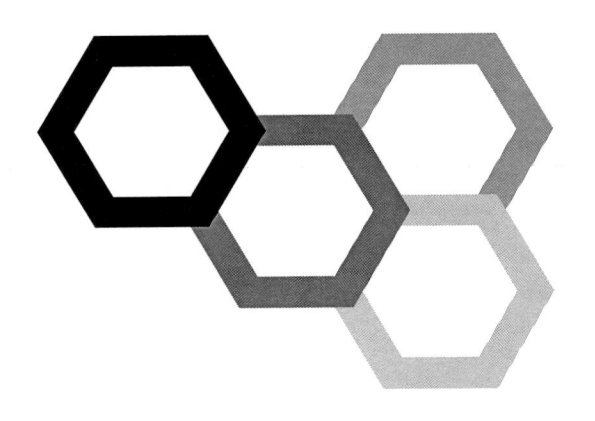

Barbara Romaine

# WRITE ARABIC NOW!

*A Handwriting Book for Letters and Words*

Handwriting by Lana Iskandarani

Georgetown University Press | Washington, DC

## Related Works

*Alif Baa: Introduction to Arabic Letters and Sounds, Third Edition*, Kristen Brustad, Mahmoud Al-Batal, and Abbas Al-Tonsi

*Al-Kitaab fii Taᶜallum al-ᶜArabiyya: A Textbook for Beginning Arabic: Part One, Third Edition*, Kristen Brustad, Mahmoud Al-Batal, and Abbas Al-Tonsi

# Contents

The publisher is not responsible for third-party websites or their content. URL links were active at time of publication.

Library of Congress Cataloging-in-Publication Data

Names: Romaine, Barbara, 1959–  author. | Iskandarani, Lana, calligrapher.
Title: Write Arabic Now! : A Handwriting Book for Letters and Words/Barbara
    Romaine ; handwriting by Lana Iskandarani.
Description: Washington, DC : Georgetown University Press, 2018.
Identifiers: LCCN 2017035589 | ISBN 9781626165687 (pbk. : alk. paper)
Subjects: LCSH: Arabic language—Writing.
Classification: LCC PJ6123 .R66 2018 | DDC 492.7/11—dc23
LC record available at https://lccn.loc.gov/2017035589

♾ This book is printed on acid-free paper meeting the requirements of the American National Standard for Permanence in Paper for Printed Library Materials.

19  18          9  8  7  6  5  4  3  2     First printing

Printed in the United States of America
Composition by click! Publishing Services
Cover design by Martha Madrid

The development of this workbook was made possible in part by a grant from the Villanova Institute for Teaching and Learning, Villanova University.

# ◇ Introduction

أَهْلاً وسهلاً—*Ahlan wa sahlan*: Welcome! Welcome to the Arabic language, and to this practical guide for learning its writing and phonetic system. It is possible that you have come to your study of the Arabic language already knowing something about it—perhaps even knowing a lot. In case this material is brand new to you, let's start with a few basics about the writing system.

Arabic is a cursive language, meaning that it is based on a system of connected letters, unlike English with its distinct printed and cursive versions. There are no upper- and lowercase letters in Arabic, but each letter does have more than one form. These forms, though similar, change according to a letter's location within a word—whether it is the first letter, somewhere in the middle, or at the end. A letter may also have a distinct form when it appears independently.

Just as English words have vowels that are identified as "short" or "long," Arabic has short and long vowels. They do not work quite the same way, though. For one thing, not all vowel sounds in Arabic are represented by letters written within the word. Only the long vowels are included. When short vowels are written, they are represented by diacritical marks above and below letters. But they are not normally written in ordinary Arabic texts because native readers have learned how to anticipate them. One objective of this workbook is to train you to do so as well. The *long* vowel in Arabic is a vowel that, when spoken, is sustained for a longer time than a short vowel. You can think of it as being held for an extra beat. In contrast, the short vowels take less time to say.

In these pages, you will work with words that are written by hand. As with other written languages, Arabic penmanship is by no means standard but varies considerably from person to person. The words provided for you in the workbook are written in a style that is as clear and regular as possible. A person dashing off a note to a friend or family member might produce nearly illegible Arabic scrawl, just as in English. For learning purposes, we want to preserve both legibility and the natural flow of a practiced hand.

As you will see, there are a great many words in these pages. This workbook is not designed to teach you vocabulary; rather, it is intended to give you extra handwriting practice, specifically with correctly forming letters and words by means of tracing exercises. The writing system of a living language is inseparably connected to the sounds of that language, and it is nearly impossible to learn how to read or write a language without clearly grasping the relationship between symbol and sound. Accordingly, these handwriting exercises are supported by an audio file, so that, as you learn to write the letters and syllables representing phonetic units (i.e., the units of sound) in the Arabic language, you can receive direct reinforcement of the correlation between what you read and write and what you hear and say.

## Getting the Most Out of This Book

The purpose of this workbook is to help you practice your handwriting in Arabic. Your focus will be on tracing the model words on each page while you listen to them on the accompanying audio. When you are ready to work independently, you can practice writing the letters and words on your own, checking them against what you see in the workbook. While it is recommended that you follow certain basic procedures, there is more than one way to use these materials to your best advantage, and you will be able to decide on some aspects of the approach you take.

Success in learning a language depends heavily on repetition, especially at the elementary level. You learned your first language by hearing—and, eventually, reading—the same words over and over again. At the same time, you gradually developed a facility for understanding meaning through grasping analogies and drawing inferences based on your perception of conceptual interconnections. Though you will develop this grasp as you gain proficiency in Arabic, effectively learning the writing system will depend substantially on rote practice. The tracing paper provided with this workbook will aid your practice as you trace words already correctly written for you, helping you get a feel for how to write the letters and letter combinations within those words accurately and smoothly.

## How to Use This Book

Every page of this workbook includes a set of instructions. These instructions are, to a certain extent, repetitive. The goal is to remind you not to omit any important steps in your work, such as the listen-and-repeat component that is crucial to cementing your understanding of Arabic. The instructions for each set of exercises are not wholly repetitive, though. Each set of directions is tailored to the particular letters being presented on that page. For this reason, you should always read the directions carefully.

With a couple of exceptions, there are seven words on a page, with each word presented four times on its practice line. In the audio accompanying these exercises, each word is repeated just twice. Of course you can listen several more times (indeed you are encouraged to do so) and repeat aloud the words you are hearing while reading and writing them.

For words with diacritics (the short vowels, for example), the instructions ask you to write them as you listen. Afterward, check your diacritical markings against the answer key, which is provided at the end of this workbook, and make any necessary corrections to your words. Please do not worry if you make mistakes in filling in the diacritics. It is to be expected that you will need some time to learn the sounds. As long as you correct your errors, you are still learning.

There is also a glossary at the back that supplies definitions for the words. Our intention is not to focus on the meanings of these words at this stage. The meanings are provided in case you are curious. A few of the words are vocabulary items that you will encounter and learn early on in your study of Arabic, but most of the words were selected to show a useful variety of letter combinations as efficiently as possible. You are free to ignore their meanings, at least for now!

This introduction to the Arabic language's beautiful writing system is only the beginning of an endeavor that—if you stay with it—promises a long and infinitely enriching adventure. Best of luck to you on your journey!

باربرا روماين

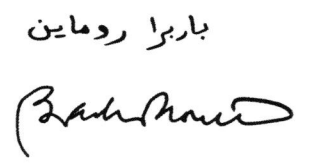

# Exercises

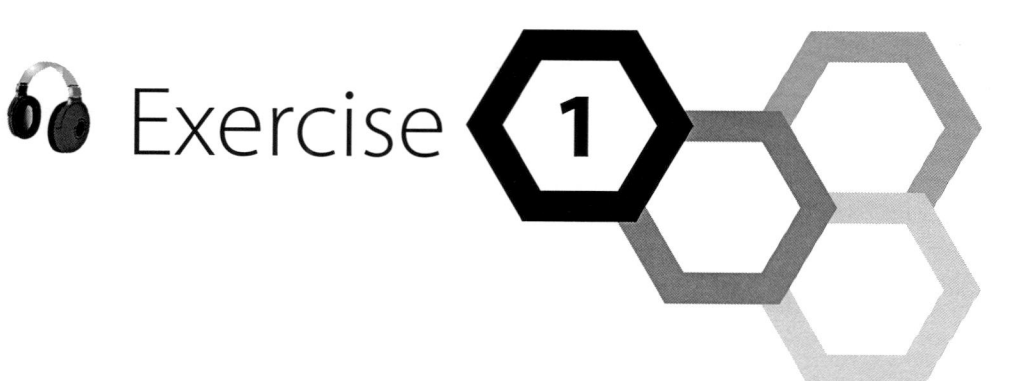

# Exercise 1

## The Consonants ب, ت, and ث

| Final | Medial | Initial | Independent |
|:---:|:---:|:---:|:---:|
| ـب | ـبـ | بـ | ب |
| ـت | ـتـ | تـ | ت |
| ـث | ـثـ | ثـ | ث |

1. Listen and write. Take care to write all dots and to position them correctly. Practice pronouncing the words as you write.
2. After tracing, listen again and add the short vowels you hear: *Damma,* (ُ ), *fatHa* (َ ), and *kasra* (ِ ).*
4. Check your work against the answer key.

   * Writing the *sukuun* (ْ ), which indicates the absence of a vowel (in words containing consonant clusters, such as تُثْبِت), is optional. When instructed to supply short vowels in these exercises, you may omit the *sukuun* if you wish.

1.

2.

3.

4.

5.

6.

7.

1

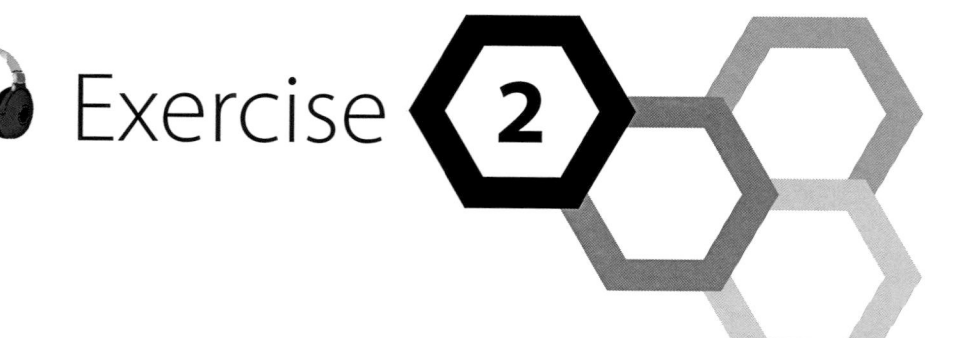

# Exercise 2

## The Long Vowel ا

| Final | Medial | Initial | Independent |
|-------|--------|---------|-------------|
| ـا | ـا | ا | ا |

1. Listen and write. Note that the letter ا is a one-way connector, meaning that it *never* connects on the left. Take care to write any dots occurring in the words you are practicing and to position them correctly. Practice pronouncing the words as you write.
2. After tracing, listen again and add the short vowels you hear: *Damma* ( ُ ), *fatHa* ( َ ), and *kasra* ( ِ ). Pay particularly close attention to the difference between the short vowel ُ and the long vowel ا.
3. Check your work against the answer key.

**2**

1. بـاتـا     بـاتـا     بـاتـا     بـاتـا

2. تـابـا     تـابـا     تـابـا     تـابـا

3. بـاتـت     بـاتـت     بـاتـت     بـاتـت

4. ثـابـت     ثـابـت     ثـابـت     ثـابـت

5. بـاث     بـاث     بـاث     بـاث

6. ثـبـات     ثـبـات     ثـبـات     ثـبـات

7. تـابـت     تـابـت     تـابـت     تـابـت

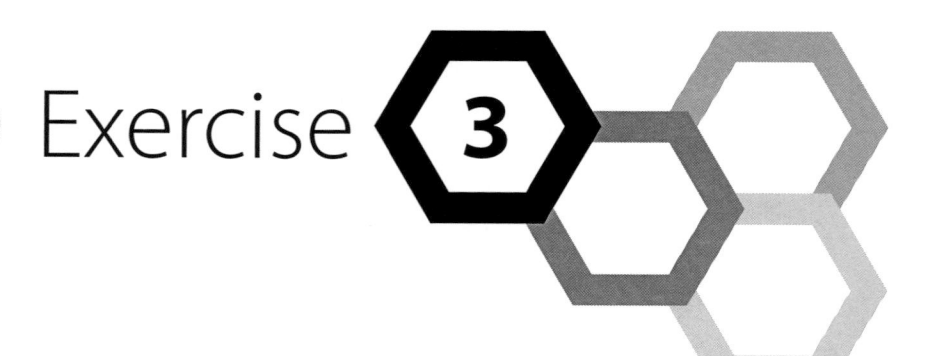

# Exercise 3

## The Long Vowels و and ي

| Final | Medial | Initial | Independent |
|-------|--------|---------|-------------|
| ـو | ـو | و | و |
| ـي | ـيـ | يـ | ي |

1. Listen and write. Though the letter و, like ا, is a one-way connector, the letter ي is a two-way connector, meaning that it can connect on either side. Take care to write all dots and to position them correctly. Practice pronouncing the words as you write.

2. After tracing, listen again and add the short vowels you hear. Pay particularly close attention to the difference between the short vowels ُ and ِ and their corresponding long vowels و and ي.

3. Check your work against the answer key.

**3**

| | | | |
|---|---|---|---|
| توبي توبي | توبي | توبي | ١. |
| بيتي بيتي | بيتي | بيتي | ٢. |
| تثوب | تثوب | تثوب | ٣. |
| ثوبي ثوبي | ثوبي | ثوبي | ٤. |
| تبيت تبيت | تبيت | تبيت | ٥. |
| ثبوت ثبوت | ثبوت | ثبوت | ٦. |
| باي باي | باي | باي | ٧. |

# Exercise ④

## The Consonants ج, ح, and خ

| Final | Medial | Initial | Independent |
|-------|--------|---------|-------------|
| ـج | ـجـ | جـ | ج |
| ـح | ـحـ | حـ | ح |
| ـخ | ـخـ | خـ | خ |

1. Listen and write. Note that these new letters are two-way connectors. Take care to write all dots and to position them correctly. Practice pronouncing the words as you write.
2. This page introduces the diphthongs. A diphthong is the effect of one vowel sound merging with another and is found in such words as ثَوْب and بَيْت (note the vowelling). Practice your pronunciation of diphthongs meticulously.
3. After tracing, listen again and add the short vowels you hear. Pay particularly close attention to the diphthongs.
4. Check your work against the answer key.

1. جبح     جبح     جبح     جبح

2. مواهب     مواهب     مواهب     مواهب

3. خبيث     خبيث     خبيث     خبيث

4. خوخ     خوخ     خوخ     خوخ

5. باحث     باحث     باحث     باحث

6. يحتاج     يحتاج     يحتاج     يحتاج

7. خيبتي     خيبتي     خيبتي     خيبتي

# Exercise 5

## The Consonants د and ذ (also introducing ء *hamza*)

| Final | Medial | Initial | Independent |
|-------|--------|---------|-------------|
| ـد | ـد | د | د |
| ـذ | ـذ | ذ | ذ |

1. Listen and write. Note that these new letters are one-way connectors. Take care to write all dots and to position them correctly. Practice pronouncing the words as you write.

2. This page also introduces the consonant *hamza* (ء), which requires ا as its seat at the beginning of a word but may stand by itself in other positions.

3. After tracing, listen again and add the short vowels you hear. Pay particularly close attention to the sound of ء: the glottal stop, or "catch in the throat."

4. Check your work against the answer key.

١. دود     دود     دود     دود

٢. أحد     أحد     أحد     أحد

٣. يجذب     يجذب     يجذب     يجذب

٤. تجويد     تجويد     تجويد     تجويد

٥. خوذتي     خوذتي     خوذتي     خوذتي

٦. جداء     جداء     جداء     جداء

٧. ذبذب     ذبذب     ذبذب     ذبذب

# Exercise 6

## The Consonants ر and ز

| Final | Medial | Initial | Independent |
|---|---|---|---|
| ـر | ـر | ر | ر |
| ـز | ـز | ز | ز |

1. Listen and write. Like د and ذ, these letters are distinguished in writing only by the presence or absence of a dot, and they are one-way connectors. Unlike د and ذ, which sit on the line, ر and ز extend below it. Take care to write all dots and to position them correctly. Pay attention to the difference in shape between ذ/د and ز/ر, with ذ/د having a sharper curve, while the curve of ز/ر is more gentle. Practice pronouncing the words as you write.
2. After tracing, listen again and add the short vowels you hear.
3. Check your work against the answer key.

**6**

| | | | |
|---|---|---|---|
| روح | روح | روح | ١. روح |
| زيادتي | زيادتي | زيادتي | ٢. زيادتي |
| خبن | خبن | خبن | ٣. خبن |
| بزوز | بزوز | بزوز | ٤. بزوز |
| ترويح | ترويح | ترويح | ٥. ترويح |
| أزباد | أزباد | أزباد | ٦. أزباد |
| ثرثار | ثرثار | ثرثار | ٧. ثرثار |

# Exercise 7

## The Consonants س and ش (also introducing ّ shadda)

| Final | Medial | Initial | Independent |
|---|---|---|---|
| ـس | ـسـ | سـ | س |
| ـش | ـشـ | شـ | ش |

1. There are two distinct ways of writing these letters by hand: (1) the "toothed" style, corresponding to the printed letters you see in books and newspapers, and (2) the "flatline" style, in which the vertical lines known as "teeth" are replaced by an elongated horizontal segment. While we emphasize the toothed style in this workbook because it is often less confusing for beginners, an example of "flatline" style can be found in the alphabet chart on pages 20–21. Eventually you may decide to adapt your own style and start writing flatline س and ش, but for these exercises, practice the toothed version.

2. Listen and write. Take care to write all dots and to position them correctly. Letters س and ش are two-way connectors. Note the crucial three dots that distinguish ش from س. Be very careful not to confuse ش with ث, which also has three dots above it but is of course an entirely different letter. Practice pronouncing the words as you write.

3. This page also presents the consonant-doubler *shadda* (ّ). Please note the following about *shadda*: (1) a consonant with a *shadda* is held for an extra beat; (2) a *shadda* <u>never</u> occurs on the first letter of a word or in combination with *sukuun* (ْ); and (3) short vowels must be written <u>above</u> *shadda*, except *kasra* (ِ), which may be written either beneath a *shadda* or beneath the relevant letter.

4. After tracing, listen again and add the short vowels you hear. Pay close attention to *shadda* and its effect on consonants. Try to notice when you hear *shadda*, and write it above the consonants on which you hear it, along with the short vowels.

5. Check your work against the answer key.

7.

6.

5.

4.

3.

2.

1.

**7**

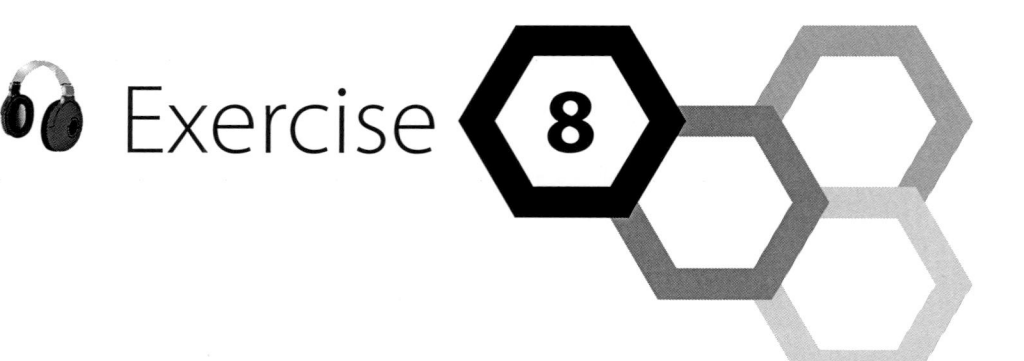

# Exercise 8

## The Consonants ص and ض

| Final | Medial | Initial | Independent |
|---|---|---|---|
| ـص | ـصـ | صـ | ص |
| ـض | ـضـ | ضـ | ض |

1. Listen and write. These letters are distinguished in writing only by the presence or absence of a dot. Always take care to write the small tooth to the left of the loop, and remember that these letters are two-way connectors. Write all dots and position them correctly. Practice pronouncing the words as you write.

2. Letters ص and ض are **emphatic consonants**, whose **nonemphatic** counterparts are س and د, respectively. Emphatic consonants have a "heavier" sound than their non-emphatic counterparts, and they tend to deepen the sounds of the surrounding vowels. Listen carefully for this deepening effect when you use the audio file for this page, and mimic it as closely as you can when you repeat the words aloud.

3. After tracing, listen again and add the short vowels you hear. Compare the sounds of the emphatic and nonemphatic consonants in the words.

4. Check your work against the answer key.

## 8

١. صرصور    صرصور    صرصور    صرصور

٢. ضرسي    ضرسي    ضرسي    ضرسي

٣. تضرج    تضرج    تضرج    تضرج

٤. تخصيص    تخصيص    تخصيص    تخصيص

٥. حوض    حوض    حوض    حوض

٦. رصاص    رصاص    رصاص    رصاص

٧. إضراب    إضراب    إضراب    إضراب

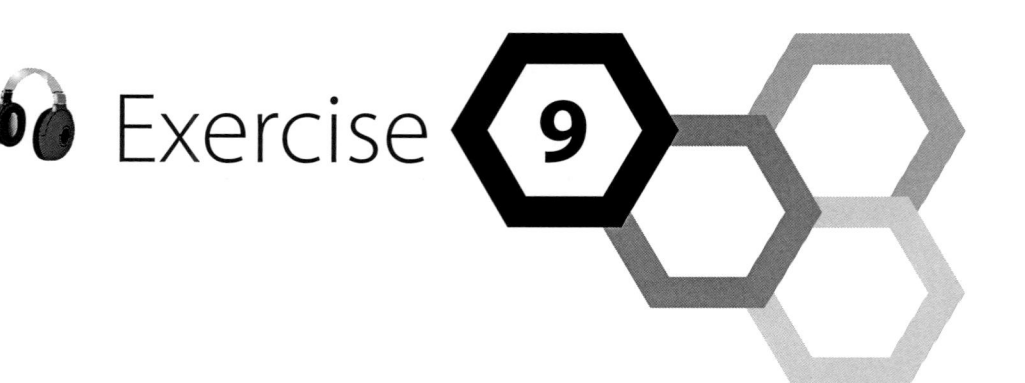

# Exercise 9

## The Consonants ط and ظ

| Final | Medial | Initial | Independent |
|:---:|:---:|:---:|:---:|
| ـط | ـطـ | طـ | ط |
| ـظ | ـظـ | ظـ | ظ |

1. Listen and write. These letters are distinguished in writing only by the presence or absence of a dot. **Note that neither ط nor ظ has a tooth,** but both feature a vertical line to the left of the loop and are two-way connectors. Observe that—like letter pairs ز/ر, د/ذ, and ص/ض—they are distinguished from each other in writing only by the presence or absence of a dot. Write all dots and position them correctly. Practice pronouncing the words as you write.

2. You have learned that ص and ض have nonemphatic counterparts س and د. Similarly, the emphatic consonants ط and ظ correspond to nonemphatic ت and ذ, respectively. Listen for the deeper vowel sounds near ط and ظ, compared to the flatter vowel sounds near ت and ذ.

3. This page also introduces the feminine marker ة/ـة, *which can only occur at the end of a word.*

4. After tracing, listen again and add the short vowels you hear. When reading aloud with the audio file and filling in diacritics (short vowels and *shaddas*), mimic as best you can the emphatic qualities of ط and ظ.

5. Check your work against the answer key.

## 9

1. طيار     طيار     طيار     طيار

2. إخطار     إخطار     إخطار     إخطار

3. ضابطة     ضابطة     ضابطة     ضابطة

4. حظيرة     حظيرة     حظيرة     حظيرة

5. حظوظ     حظوظ     حظوظ     حظوظ

6. ش ط ط     ش ط ط     ش ط ط     ش ط ط

7. ظباء     ظباء     ظباء     ظباء

# Arabic Alphabet

Forms of the twenty-eight principal letters:

| Final | Medial | Initial | Independent |
|:---:|:---:|:---:|:---:|
| ﺎ | ﺎ | ا | ا |
| ﺐ | ﺒ | ﺑ | ب |
| ﺖ | ﺘ | ﺗ | ت |
| ﺚ | ﺜ | ﺛ | ث |
| ﺞ | ﺠ | ﺟ | ج |
| ﺢ | ﺤ | ﺣ | ح |
| ﺦ | ﺨ | ﺧ | خ |
| ﺪ | ﺪ | ﺩ | د |
| ﺬ | ﺬ | ﺫ | ذ |
| ﺮ | ﺮ | ﺭ | ر |
| ﺰ | ﺰ | ﺯ | ز |
| ﺲ / ﺲ | ﺴ / ﺴ | ﺳ / ﺳ | ﺱ / ﺱ |
| ﺶ / ﺶ * | ﺸ / ﺸ | ﺷ / ﺷ | ﺵ / ﺵ |
| ﺺ | ﺼ | ﺻ | ص |
| ﺾ | ﻀ | ﺿ | ض |

\* Regarding ﺱ and ﺵ: Two versions of each letter are shown here, one of which we call "toothed" (the vertical segments are the "teeth") and the other "flatline." Because flatline ﺱ and ﺵ are commonly used in handwritten Arabic, it is important that you be familiar with them, although in this workbook we are asking you to write the toothed version, which tends to be clearer for beginners. Once you have mastered the basic Arabic writing system it will be up to you to decide whether or not you wish to switch to flatline ﺱ and ﺵ.

| Final | Medial | Initial | Independent |
|---|---|---|---|
| ط | ط | ط | ط |
| ظ | ظ | ظ | ظ |
| ع | ع | ع | ع |
| غ | غ | غ | غ |
| ف | ف | ف | ف |
| ق | ق | ق | ق |
| ك | ك | ك | ك |
| ل | ل | ل | ل |
| م | م | م | م |
| ن | ن | ن | ن |
| ه | ه | ه | ه |
| و | و | و | و |
| ي | ي | ي | ي |

# Exercise 10

## The Consonants ع and غ

| Final | Medial | Initial | Independent |
|:---:|:---:|:---:|:---:|
| ـع | ـعـ | عـ | ع |
| ـغ | ـغـ | غـ | غ |

1. Listen and write these letters, which are two-way connectors. Take care to write all dots and to position them correctly. Practice pronouncing the words as you write. It's extremely important to learn to distinguish ع and غ—both in the sounds they represent and in how they are written—from ح and خ. This confusion happens often, so pay special attention to the pronunciation and proper formation of these letters.

2. When written in medial and final positions, ع and غ are not rounded the way they are in independent and initial positions: they are *pointy*. In fact, the body of letters ع and غ in medial and final positions should look similar to an inverted triangle. If you form them as smooth loops instead of as pointy triangles, they will resemble other letters. When you see the inverted triangle of medial and final ع and غ in print, you may notice that the centers of the letters are most often solid (i.e., filled in like this ـعـ ), but in handwritten form they may be open (not filled in: ـعـ ). For For the purposes of this workbook, we are leaving them open.

3. After tracing, listen again and add the short vowels you hear. Because the sounds of ع and غ differ considerably from English, you should give extra effort to identifying the short vowels associated with them.

4. Check your work against the answer key, which should help you get the hang of short vowels with ع and غ.

**10**

1.

2.

3.

4.

5.

6.

7.

# Exercise 11

## The Consonants ف and ق

| Final | Medial | Initial | Independent |
|:---:|:---:|:---:|:---:|
| ـف | ـفـ | فـ | ف |
| ـق | ـقـ | قـ | ق |

1. Listen and write these letters, which are both two-way connectors. Take care to write all dots and to position them correctly. Practice pronouncing the words as you write. With ق you should notice the deepening of associated vowels, both long and short, that occurs with emphatic consonants.

2. Note that ف and ق are distinguished in writing not only by the number of dots but also by their shapes when written in independent and final positions. In these two positions, ق drops well *below* the line (ـق), whereas ف sits directly *on* the line (ـف).

3. After tracing, listen again and add the short vowels you hear.

4. Check your work against the answer key.

١. فريق    فريق    فريق    فريق

٢. غفوة    غفوة    غفوة    غفوة

٣. يقرر    يقرر    يقرر    يقرر

٤. زفاف    زفاف    زفاف    زفاف

٥. فوق    فوق    فوق    فوق

٦. قريبة    قريبة    قريبة    قريبة

٧. أقف    أقف    أقف    أقف

## The Consonants ك and ل

| Final | Medial | Initial | Independent |
|-------|--------|---------|-------------|
| ـك | ـكـ | كـ | ك |
| ـل | ـلـ | لـ | ل |

1. Listen and write these letters, which are both two-way connectors. Take care to write any dots occurring in the words you are practicing and position them correctly. Practice pronouncing the words as you write.

2. Make sure that you connect ل on the left when it occurs in initial or medial position, and make sure, in independent and final positions, to give it its full shape—like a "hook" that drops below the line. If you omit this hook, a ل ends up looking like an ا ! Note that ل takes a special shape when it is immediately followed by an ا, combining the two letters thus: لا. The ا is written as a leftward-angled stroke tucked into the curve of the ل: ا + ل = لا. Since the ا is the second letter in the sequence and ا is a one-way connector, nothing can connect on the left of the لا combination, although it can connect on the right, as in the word حَلال.

3. The letter ك sits on the line in all of its positions, unlike ل. To avoid confusing ك with ل, it is important to remember that the *hamza* embellishes ك in its independent and final forms, and that the crossbar characterizes its initial and medial forms.

4. After tracing, listen again and add the short vowels you hear.

5. Check your work against the answer key.

**12**

لقد     لقد     لقد     لقد .1

قلبك     قلبك     قلبك     قلبك .2

كلاب     كلاب     كلاب     كلاب .3

أشكل     أشكل     أشكل     أشكل .4

حياك     حياك     حياك     حياك .5

إقفال     إقفال     إقفال     إقفال .6

يكيلد     يكيلد     يكيلد     يكيلد .7

## The Consonants م and ن

| Final | Medial | Initial | Independent |
|:---:|:---:|:---:|:---:|
| ـم | ـمـ | مـ | م |
| ـن | ـنـ | نـ | ن |

1. Listen and write these letters, which are both two-way connectors. Take care to write all dots and to position them correctly. Practice pronouncing the words as you write.

2. The body of م should be smaller than that of ف or of ق. Unlike medial and final ع and غ, medial م is rounded, not triangular. While some writers fill in the loop that forms م , we leave it open.

3. The basic appearance of the letter ن in initial and medial positions—featuring an upright segment, or "tooth"—resembles that of ب, ت, and ث. Its independent and final form, however, differs in shape and in the fact that its body drops *below* the line, whereas the bodies of ب, ت, and ث sit *on* the line in all positions. Remember to place the dot *above* ن and not *beneath* it.

4. After tracing, listen again and add the short vowels you hear. These letters correspond closely to English "m" and "n," so accurately mimicking the sounds should be relatively easy.

5. Check your work against the answer key.

## 13

1. مواضيع     مواضيع     مواضيع     مواضيع

2. نيران     نيران     نيران     نيران

3. لمسة     لمسة     لمسة     لمسة

4. تعوفين     تعوفين     تعوفين     تعوفين

5. حنين     حنين     حنين     حنين

6. يليم     يليم     يليم     يليم

7. كمناء     كمناء     كمناء     كمناء

# Exercise 14

## The Consonant ـه

| Final | Medial | Initial | Independent |
|:---:|:---:|:---:|:---:|
| ـه | ـهـ | هـ | ه |

1. Listen and write this letter, which is a two-way connector. Take care to write any dots in the words you are practicing and position them correctly. Practice pronouncing the words as you write. Unlike letter ح (presented earlier), which is produced from farther back in the throat, ـه resembles the English "h." One of the sample words on this page—أحبه—contains both ـه and ح; listen for the difference between the two "h" sounds.

2. There are various styles of writing medial ـهـ. The version that looks like an icicle hanging down beneath the line is the simplest. Note also that independent and final ـه are identical in shape to the two forms of ة but that ـه has no dots.

3. After tracing, listen again and add the short vowels you hear. Practice saying أحبه several times aloud and try to feel in your throat the difference between ـه and ح.

4. Check your work against the answer key.

## 14

1. هوامة هوامة هوامة هوامة

2. تهرمون تهرمون تهرمون تهرمون

3. كريه كريه كريه كريه

4. عيناه عيناه عيناه عيناه

5. هيكل هيكل هيكل هيكل

6. أحبه أحبه أحبه أحبه

7. يهربون يهربون يهربون يهربون

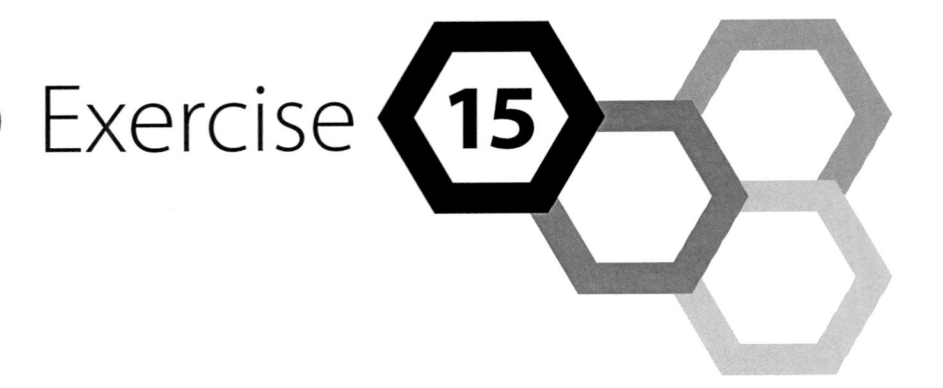

# Exercise 15

## The Definite Article ‎ال and Words with Dagger *alif* (ّ◌)

1. Listen and write the definite article, ‎ال, and the variant of the letter *alif* known as dagger *alif* ◌ّ. Take care to write any dots occurring in the words you are practicing and position them correctly. Practice pronouncing the words as you write. For pronunciation, review the rules for sun and moon letters. Pay close attention to the characteristics of sun and moon letters with ‎ال, doing your best to mimic them accurately.

2. The article ‎ال can feature a number of stylistic variations, but we have not represented them here. It is useful to be able to recognize them, however, as they occur frequently. The *laam* in the combination sometimes stacks atop the letter that follows, as in ‎الحب (where ‎ل sits atop ‎ح). Another common convention is the placement of ‎م such that it is tucked in to the right of the ‎ل, and can be easy to miss. It may appear as if it precedes ‎ل rather than following it, like so: ‎المر .

   Although the dagger *alif* (◌ّ) is pronounced and sounds like a regular *alif*, it is often omitted in writing. When it is written, the letters on either side follow the normal rules for connection or nonconnection, just as if the dagger *alif* were not there.

3. After tracing, listen again and add the short vowels you hear.

4. Check your work against the answer key.

١. الحبيب   الحبيب   الحبيب   الحبيب

٢. اللغة   اللغة   اللغة   اللغة

٣. الأُصول   الأُصول   الأُصول   الأُصول

٤. هٰذا/هٰذه   هٰذا/هٰذه   هٰذا/هٰذه   هٰذا/هٰذه

٥. السماء   السماء   السماء   السماء

٦. الإشارة   الإشارة   الإشارة   الإشارة

٧. اللامع   اللامع   اللامع   اللامع

# Exercise 16

## Words containing *alif maadda* (آ); other variations on *hamza*

| Final | Medial | Initial | Independent |
|:---:|:---:|:---:|:---:|
| ﺎ | ﺎ | أ | أ |
| ﻮﺆ | ﻮﺆ | ؤ | ؤ |
| ﺊ | ﺌ | ﺋ | ئ |

1. Listen and write these letters in various combinations. Take care to write any dots that occur in the words you are practicing and position them correctly. Practice pronouncing the words as you write. As you listen, observe and imitate the pronunciation of *hamza*, and notice that *alif maadda* (آ) is effectively a hamza variation, equivalent to *hamza + alif*: that is, the glottal stop immediately followed by the sound of long-vowel *alif*, as in the word آنِسة ('*aanisa*) or the word قُرآن (*Qur'aan*). Notice that *hamza* and *alif maadda* can occur anywhere in a word and that in formal Arabic the glottal stop is distinctly pronounced, even in the middle or at the end of a word. This phenomenon is essentially nonexistent in standard English, except in the slang word "uh-oh."

2. As a reminder, *hamza* is phonetically a glottal stop (or "catch in the throat") written in various ways, including when it is seated on و (ؤ/ؤ—) or on ي (ﺊ/ﺌ/ﺋ). These exercises give you an extra opportunity to practice writing *hamza* while listening to how it is pronounced in a word. The "seating" of *hamza* takes time and effort to learn, so do not worry if it takes you a while to get it right.

3. This exercise also contains an example of *alif maqSuura* (ى), the "squashed *alif*," which is pronounced like regular *alif* despite looking like a ي missing its dots. The *alif maqSuura* can only occur at the end of a word.

4. After tracing, listen again and add the short vowels you hear.

5. Check your work against the answer key.

## 16

1. براءة       براءة       براءة       براءة

2. تفاؤل       تفاؤل       تفاؤل       تفاؤل

3. المتشائم    المتشائم    المتشائم    المتشائم

4. متآكل       متآكل       متآكل       متآكل

5. يأتي        يأتي        يأتي        يأتي

6. مؤدى        مؤدى        مؤدى        مؤدى

7. سئلت        سئلت        سئلت        سئلت

Exercise 16 Practice!

# Exercise 17

## The Particles بِ and لِ

1. Listen and write the words containing these particles. Take care to write all dots and to position them correctly. Practice pronouncing the words as you write. As you listen and write, remember the rule that the combination of ال + لِ is always written لل. This is, essentially, a spelling exception. Pay very close attention to, and carefully mimic, the pronunciation of words preceded by بِ or لِ, with or without the definite article ال.

2. After tracing, listen again and add the short vowels you hear.

3. Check your work against the answer key.

## 17

1. بالقطار    بالقطار    بالقطار    بالقطار

2. للإمام    للإمام    للإمام    للإمام

3. بطريقة    بطريقة    بطريقة    بطريقة

4. لأختها    لأختها    لأختها    لأختها

5. بالليل    بالليل    بالليل    بالليل

6. للشاعر    للشاعر    للشاعر    للشاعر

7. بقلم أمي    بقلم أمي    بقلم أمي    بقلم أمي

Practice

1. قاضٍ

2. الإمارة

3. جامعة

4. قاضيه

5. المستقيم

6. أهلًا

7. الجبال

## Answer Key and Glossary

### Exercise 1

| | |
|---|---:|
| settlement, decision | بَت |
| he/it perished, was destroyed | تَب |
| he/it spread, unrolled, unfolded | بَث |
| reliable, trustworthy | ثَبَت |
| annihilation | تَبَب |
| you (f. sing.) repented | تُبْتِ |
| after negating particle *lam*: you (m. sing.) [didn't] return | تَثُب |

### Exercise 2

| | |
|---|---:|
| they two spent the night | باتا |
| they two repented | تابا |
| she spent the night | باتَت |
| fixed, immovable | ثابِت |
| Bath (city of) | باث |
| firmness, stability | ثَبات |
| she repented | تابَت |

### Exercise 3

| | |
|---|---:|
| repent! (f. sing.) | توبـي |
| spend the night! (f. sing.) | بيتي |
| she returns/you (m. sing.) return | تَثوب |

| | |
|---|---|
| return! (f. sing.) | ثوبـي |
| she spends/you (m. sing.) spend the night | تَبيت |
| constancy, immutability | ثُبـوت |
| Bey | باي |

## Exercise 4

| | |
|---|---|
| beehive | جَبْح |
| eyebrows | حَواجِب |
| wicked, malicious | خَبيث |
| peaches | خَوْخ |
| researcher | باحِـث |
| he needs | يَحْتاج |
| my disappointment | خَيْبَتـي |

## Exercise 5

| | |
|---|---|
| worms | دود |
| one, (some)one, (any)one | أَحَد |
| he/it attracts | يَجذِب |
| melodic recitation of the Qur'an | تَجْـويد |
| my helmet | خوذَتـي |
| kids, young goats | جداء |
| he set swinging, set in a swinging motion | ذَبْذَب |

## Exercise 6

| | |
|---|---|
| spirit | روح |
| my increase, my surplus | زِيادَتـي |
| bread | خُبْز |

| | |
|---|---|
| linens, fabrics | بُزوز |
| fanning, aeration | تَرْويح |
| foam bubbles | أَزْباد |
| chatterbox, prattler | ثَرْثار |

## Exercise 7

| | |
|---|---|
| she will visit/you (m. sing.) will visit | سَتَزور |
| bribery | رَشْو |
| worshipper | سَجّاد |
| professor | أُسْتاذ |
| purchase, buying | شِراء |
| flowing, streaming | بَجيس |
| slate | شِسْت |

## Exercise 8

| | |
|---|---|
| cricket | صُرصور |
| my molar | ضِرسي |
| he/it reddened, became red | تَضَرَّج |
| specification, designation | تَخْصيص |
| basin | حَوْض |
| lead (metal) | رَصاص |
| strike, sit-in | إضْراب |

## Exercise 9

| | |
|---|---|
| pilot | طَيّار |
| notification, information | إخْطار |
| female officer | ضابِطة |

| | |
|---|---|
| enclosure, pen | حَظيرة |
| protrusion, bulge | جُحوظ |
| excess | شَطَط |
| gazelles | ظِباء |

## Exercise 10

| | |
|---|---|
| female Arab | عَرَبِيَّة |
| copious (f.) | غَزيرَة |
| distant; wide | شاسِع |
| curves, twists, turns | تَعاريج |
| headache | صُداع |
| front teeth; inlets | ثُغور |
| nursling, newborn | رَضيع |

## Exercise 11

| | |
|---|---|
| team | فَريق |
| nap, snooze | غَفْوَة |
| he decides | يُقَرِّر |
| wedding processional | زِفاف |
| above | فَوْق |
| near (f.) | قَريبَة |
| I stop, I stand | أَقِف |

## Exercise 12

| | |
|---|---|
| past-tense connecting particle | لَقَد |
| your (m. sing.) heart | قَلْبُكَ |
| dogs | كِلاب |

| I hobble [someone or something] | أَشْكُل |
| weave, weaving | حِياك |
| locking, shutting | إِقْفال |
| they two (m.) measure (subjunctive) | يَكيلا |

## Exercise 13

| topics | مَواضيع |
| fires | نيـران |
| a touch | لَمْسَة |
| you (f. sing.) float | تَعومين |
| longing, desire, nostalgia | حَنين |
| he curses, censures | يُليم |
| hidden, lying in ambush (m. pl.) | كُمَناء |

## Exercise 14

| pigeon, dove | هَمامَة |
| you all grow old, senescent | تَهْرَمون |
| hateful, repugnant | كَريه |
| his eyes | عَيْناهُ |
| skeleton, framework | هَيْكَل |
| he loved him/it | أَحَبَّهُ |
| they (m. pl.) smuggle | يُهَرِّبون |

## Exercise 15

| the beloved (m. sing.) | الحَبيب |
| the language | اللُغَة |
| the origins | الأُصول |

| | |
|---|---|
| this (masc./fem.) | هٰذا/هٰذِهِ |
| the sky | السَّماء |
| the signal | الإشارَة |
| the shining | اللامِع |

## Exercise 16

| | |
|---|---|
| innocence | بَراءَة |
| optimism | تَفاؤُل |
| the pessimist | الـمُتَشائِم |
| corroded | مُتَآكِل |
| he/it comes | يَأْتـي |
| assignment; purport | مُؤَدّى |
| I was asked | سُئِلْتُ |

## Exercise 17

| | |
|---|---|
| by (the) train | بِالقِطار |
| for/to the imam | لِلإمام |
| by way of | بِطَريقَة |
| to/for her sister | لِأُخْتِها |
| at night | بِاللَّيْل |
| for/to the poet | لِلشّاعِر |
| by my mother's pen/= written by my mother | بِقَلَم أُمّي |

## Practice

| | |
|---|---|
| your (m. sing.) heart | قَلْبُكَ |
| the signal | الإشارَة |
| topics | مَواضيع |

| | |
|---|---|
| female officer | ضابِطة |
| the pessimist | الـمُتَشائِم |
| by my mother's pen/= written by my mother | بِقَلَم أُمّي |
| by (the) train | بِالقِطار |

## About Barbara Romaine

Barbara Romaine has been teaching the Arabic language since the early 1990s and publishing her translations of Arabic literature (novels, short stories, and poetry) for nearly as long. She has held two NEA fellowships in translation, placed second in the Banipal Saif-Ghobash competition in 2011 for her translation of Radwa Ashour's *Specters*, and her translations of Abbasid poetry recently published in *Pusteblume* have been nominated for a Pushcart Prize. Barbara has taught at institutions along the Eastern Seaboard from Virginia to Vermont, and has taught at Villanova University since 2008.

## About Lana Iskandarani

Born and raised in the Syrian capital of Damascus, Lana Iskandarani experienced a multicultural upbringing with Mediterranean influences. In 1996 Lana and her family immigrated to the United States where she obtained her master of education at Arcadia University with a concentration in Connected Learning. Lana has taught Arabic in the United States for twenty years, and has taught at West Chester University since 2010.